Turtl[...]

by[...]

Professional Breeders Series™

E C O

© 2005 by ECO Herpetological Publishing & Distribution.

ISBN 978-0-9767334-6-3

Copies available from:

ECO Herpetological Publishing & Distribution
915 Seymour Lansing, MI 48906 USA
telephone: 517.487.5595   fax: 517.371.2709
e-mail: ecoorders@hotmail.com   website: http://www.reptileshirts.com

T-Rex Products, Inc.
http://www.t-rexproducts.com

Zoo Book Sales
http://www.zoobooksales.com

LIVING ART publishing
http://www.livingartpublishing.com

Design and layout by Russ Gurley.
Cover design by Rafael Porrata.

Printed in China.

Front Cover: The beautiful Midland Painted Turtle, *Chrysemys picta marginata*. Photo by Russ Gurley.
Back Cover: The Matamata, *Chelus fimbriatus*. Photo by Bill Love.

INTRODUCTION

The keeping of turtles is a fast-growing and exciting branch of herpetoculture. Turtles, once a common household pet, are returning to homes, this time accompanied by a new bank of knowledge pertaining to their needs and new excitement revolving around their care in captivity. Turtles are under incredible pressure in the natural world. Their habitats are disappearing, their environments are being poisoned and fragmented, and they are being eaten in record numbers. The proper care of turtles in captive situations is more important now than ever before. We, as keepers, are obliged to learn all we can about our turtles and to share this knowledge not only with other turtle keepers, but to anyone who will listen about our beloved chelonians and what they mean to us and to the natural world. We take on the responsibility of keeping our turtles healthy and providing them with creative and thoughtful captive enclosures that not only meet their needs, but also keep them fit and stimulated.

As turtle breeders enjoy more success, turtles are available in ever increasing numbers. Species from around the world are being offered by breeders at shows and through their breeding facilities. For most of these turtles, the initial week or two are critical. They require thoughtful care and a clean, warm environment with their specific needs met. In this book, I am excited to present information and ideas that can help keepers provide the appropriate captive environment for their turtles.

I hope that *Turtles in Captivity* will offer helpful and practical information to help you properly care for, and most importantly, enjoy your pet turtle.

Russ Gurley
Director
Turtle and Tortoise Preservation Group
http://www.ttpg.org

ACKNOWLEDGEMENTS

A special thank you to the turtle keepers and breeders who have not only welcomed me to visit and photograph their facilities and animals but who are inspiring turtle keepers worlwide. Thanks to Wayne Hill, Dennis Uhrig, Paul vander Schouw, George Ullmann, Elmar Meier, Al Weinberg, Marc Cantos, Kurt Edwards, and Rusty Mills for providing turtles and enclosures to photograph and thanks to Bill Love of Blue Chameleon Ventures for providing some of his excellent images.

TABLE OF CONTENTS

Chapter ONE: **Choosing a Turtle**

The hardy and prolific Red-eared Slider (*Trachemys elegans*) has become the most widespread turtle species in the world from people turning loose their unwanted pets. This is an ecological disaster in many natural areas. Photo by Russ Gurley.

Is a Turtle Right For You?

To be quite honest, this book has not been written to promote the widespread keeping of turtles as pets. Actually, for most people, turtles are lousy pets and keeping them can end up being a bad experience for both the keeper and the turtle. Most aquatic turtles get large and they require expensive enclosures in which to live. Despite childhood memories of the plastic turtle bowl with palm tree, most turtles will require large enclosures with plenty of clean, filtered water. Water cleanliness, filtration, aeration, and water temperature are very important for the well-being of most species of turtles. In addition, turtles require sunlight or its approximation through expensive UVB-emitting bulbs. All turtles must have variety in their diets, some requiring up to a dozen different foods each week. Most young turtles require the addition of live food such as earthworms, redworms, crickets, and small fish to their diet. These dietary needs will require trips to the local pet store or bait shop or will require you to have live insects shipped to your home from invertebrate dealers.

Turtle enclosures, especially elaborate outdoor enclosures, can be expensive to build and maintain. However, having a fascinating piece of the natural world in your life makes them well worthwhile. Courtesy of School of the Plains, Oklahoma City. Photo by Russ Gurley.

For children wanting a reptile pet, we recommend a cornsnake or a leopard gecko. Turtles and tortoises generally require a lot of research and some experience with the needs of sun-loving reptile pets. For those willing to invest the time, energy, and financial commitment, turtles can be very rewarding on many levels. If a turtle's needs are not met properly, it can be a wholly frustrating disappointment. Read, question, explore, and weigh your realistic abilities, physically, financially, and emotionally, and if you decide to enter the world of turtle keeping, this book should be helpful in beginning your journey.

Finding a Turtle

After choosing to keep a turtle, and designing and preparing the proper enclosure, the next step is the search for a healthy specimen.

Captive-hatched turtles such as these Argentine Side-necked Turtles, *Phrynops hilarii*, thrive in proper enclosures. Photo by Russ Gurley.

Captive-hatched Specimens

Captive-hatched baby turtles are typically healthy, alert, and somewhat accustomed to human presence. With thoughtful care, they will eat well, grow quickly, and become wonderful pets. There is a growing trend in the reptile hobby for pet stores and reptile dealers to offer only captive-hatched turtles to those wanting a pet turtle. Captive-hatched turtles are an ever-increasing part of our hobby. This is an exciting trend.

There are many positive reasons to buy small captive-hatched specimens . . . With new knowledge of nutrition and the benefits of varied diets, captive-hatched babies can grow faster and healthier, reaching breeding size much sooner. Turtles produced in captivity are unlikely to have parasites. They will tend to experience little or no stress during handling. There is also the simple fact of necessity - In many cases, the only way for

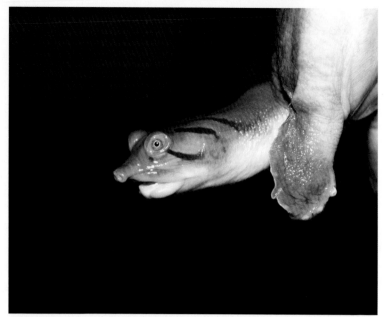

Some species are nearly non-existent in the hobby of turtle-keeping, even as captive-hatched specimens. This is *Aspideretes gangeticus*, the Ganges Soft-shelled Turtle. Photo by Russ Gurley.

keepers to obtain some of the rarest species is for them to buy captive-hatched turtles from another turtle breeder who has been fortunate enough to establish and to breed an unusual or rare species.

Places to Find Captive-hatched Turtles

Pet and Specialty Stores

As interest grows, more and more pet stores are offering turtles for sale. Not only are they offering turtles for pets, but they are exhibiting healthy animals in proper and inspiring setups. Many are offering correct advice and stocking the best equipment and supplies for their customers. In the past, many pet stores did not establish proper enclosures to keep turtles long-term. Filtration was absent or inefficient and specimens were often in poor health and species from all over the world were mixed together in a single, large turtle tank. As imported specimens made up most of the turtles for sale in the shops, most were traumatized and parasitized.

Now, with the increased emphasis on the true needs of turtles, shops are installing larger enclosures with filtration and basking spots. They are using better food and many are even offering veterinary services to properly care for turtles before or during sales times.

Though many continue to get a bad rap, these shops are literally the front line in our crusade to educate the general public about turtles. As the first stop for most people searching for a pet turtle, pet stores have the unique ability to inspire a beginning turtle keeper's first creative ideas and to offer proper procedures for setting up and caring for animals.

Shows and Expos

In recent years, reptile shows and expos have popped up all over the country. In the last few years there has been an increase in the number of captive-produced baby turtles at these

Captive breeding programs are producing healthy, stress-free specimens for hobbyists. This is a hatching Florida Box Turtle, *Terrapene bauri*. Photo by Russ Gurley.

This young Diamondback Terrapin, *Malaclemys terrapin*, appears alert and strong. Photo by Russ Gurley.

shows. The country's top shows include the National Reptile Breeders Expo and the NARBC shows in Anaheim, Chicago, and Philadelphia. There are also many other very good regional shows around the United States. Typically the specimens offered at these shows are healthy, feeding well, and are excellent specimens to begin a turtle-keeping hobby or to add to an existing collection. At these shows you get the rare opportunity to hand-pick the turtles you want to purchase and you often have the opportunity to speak with the breeder. When having turtles shipped to you, there is always the risk of receiving turtles that are picked by someone who may not have your best interest at heart. Add to the savings of not having to pay shipping and the lack of stress placed on the animals from shipping and the shows and expos are an excellent opportunity to get some really nice turtles.

Turtle Breeders

Some keepers are fortunate to have a local turtle breeder near their home. Often, these breeders will welcome visitors

Turtle breeders often have large enclosures that ensure natural behaviors such as mating and egg-laying. Courtesy of George Ullmann. Photo by Russ Gurley.

(potential customers) to their facilities. In this situation, you get to see the breeder's facilities and see his or her animals. You might learn some of their tricks, glean some experience and helpful hints from them, and often gain a new friend or colleague with whom to share ideas and offspring. You can find these breeders through a local herp society, ads in a reptile magazine, or on the Internet.

The Internet

The Internet has developed into a source of live animals. There are several extensive websites that offer classified ad sections where one can buy animals and plants as well as ponds, pumps, filters, food, and more. There have unfortunately been occasional problems with unscrupulous, faceless dealers. When buying this way, one doesn't get to see the animals or the facilities, and many of these Internet dealers are simply buying and reselling animals. Some don't disclose to beginners that an animal is captive-produced or wild-caught, or even worse, lie and say that it is when it isn't. There are also concerns about shipping, even with overnight delivery services. There are Styrofoam-lined boxes, disposable heat packs, and most boxes can travel across the country in a day without a problem. We try to only ship and receive turtles from April to October and are careful during cold nights in winter and hot days in summer.

If you are careful and inquisitive, these Internet dealers can be a good source for turtles. When you contact dealers selling turtles, ask plenty of questions. These people want to sell you a live turtle (or turtles) and keep you as a future customer so they should be willing to spend a little extra time with you. Make sure they are charging a fair price by looking around at what these animals typically sell for in other ads and from other sources such as dealer price lists. Do your homework. Most will be willing to send you photos of the specific animal in which you are interested. Find out about their packing and shipping techniques. Make sure they sound legal, logical, and safe for the animal. If the seller is rude or unwilling to answer your questions, move on and count your blessings. Typically, these deals end up being the ones you regret.

Choosing a Specific Turtle

When you discover a turtle that you are interested in purchasing, whether at a pet store or reptile show, begin by checking out the turtle's enclosure. If it is an aquatic species, check the water. It should be relatively clean and turtles should not be crowded. If it is a terrestrial species, check its water dish. It should be clean and free of any feces or dead insects. If turtles from different parts of the world are kept together, especially in crowded conditions, we suggest you don't buy any.

Ask about the turtle that has caught your eye. If captive-hatched, was it bred by the person you are talking to? Was it bred locally? What's it been through over the last few days?

Pick up the turtle: It should be alert and active.

Check its weight: It should be heavy.

Check its strength: It should push off of your fingers with force.

Check its uniformity: The shape of the scutes should be regular and there should be no noticeable bumps, lumps, or asymmetry to its body.

Strong, hard, and blemish-free shells are important characteristics to closely notice when choosing a young turtle. These are *Phrynops tuberosus*. Photo by Russ Gurley.

Check its eyes: They should be open, clear, mucus-free, and alert.

Check its nostrils: The nostrils should be open and free from any bubbles or discharge.

Check its mouth: The mouth should be free from injuries, irregularities, or lumps.

Check its vent: Its cloacal opening and tail should be free of any discharge or lumps.

Ask about any guarantee the seller might offer. Is this guarantee offered in writing? Remember, you are often stuck with your decision with no possibility of a refund. In fairness, the seller can't know your home's conditions or the care you will offer and so can only guarantee the turtle's current health.

Chapter TWO: Your Turtle's New Home

A standard 20-gallon long aquarium (30" x 12" x 12") with a filter, heater, and heat lamp over a basking area, provide an ideal home for young turtles. Photo by Russ Gurley.

Once you've purchased your turtle, it will be ready for its new enclosure. These first few days of a life in its new surroundings are crucial.

An incandescent bulb in a clamp-on fixture provides a basking spot and helps keep this blackwater turtle enclosure warm. Photo by Russ Gurley.

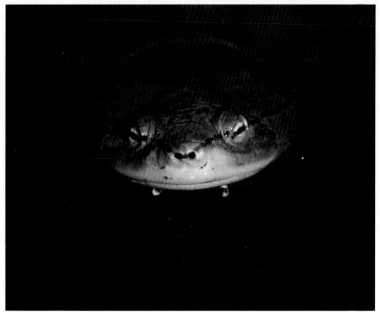

Some aquatic species such as this Argentine Side-necked Turtle, *Phrynops hilarii*, get quite large as adults. Photo by Russ Gurley.

If a suitable enclosure and well thought out plan are not in place, sensitive species can go downhill and even die very quickly. Spend time designing and setting up a proper enclosure for your turtle before it arrives at your home.

Aquatic Species

The Enclosure

The first home for hatchling aquatic turtles can be a glass aquarium. Aquariums are easy to find at your local pet store or at a reptile show. A 10-gallon (20"*l* x 10"*w* x 12"*h*) aquarium, a 20-gallon long aquarium (30"*l* x 12"*w* x 12"*h*), or a similarly sized plastic tub work well for small turtles. In these first weeks, smaller enclosures allow young turtles easier access to food. (Most successful keepers suggest that you have 6" of enclosure for every 1" of baby turtle.)

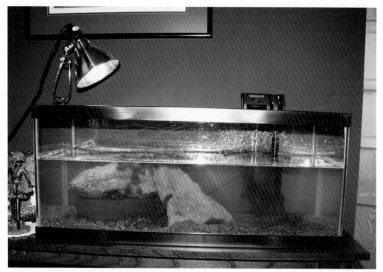

This enclosure - a 20-gallon long aquarium - provides for all of a small aquatic turtle's needs. Photo by Russ Gurley.

An inch or two of washed sand can be added to the enclosure. This substrate will hold aquatic plants and will give your turtle a place to dig and to explore for food.

A sturdy land area for basking should be established by the addition of a piece of bark, cork bark, driftwood, or pieces of slate.

The Water

Clean, chlorine-free water should be added to the depth of at least twice the length of the turtle's top shell, or carapace. If the water is too shallow, the turtle may flip over and be unable to right itself and drown. Deeper water allows the turtle to swim itself right side up. In these early days, swimming no doubt serves to strengthen their muscles as well. The water is obviously an important part of a turtle's environment and the attention a keeper gives to the water will often mean the difference between success and disappointment.

Water Conditions

Chlorine

The addition of a chlorine (or chloramine) remover is an important first step in preparing the water for your captive turtles. There are many products to remove chlorine and chloramines on the market. These are available from your local pet store.

pH and Water Hardness

Typically pH and water hardness are not as important for a captive-hatched turtle's health. In fact, most captive-hatched turtles seem tolerant of a range of water conditions. Water cleanliness and water temperature, however, are very important to the long-term health of your turtle.

Several South American species will need to be kept in acidic (5.0 to 5.5) water to ensure their health. A keeper

This large, blackwater system provides the ideal home for young Matamata Turtles (*Chelus fimbriatus*). Photo by Russ Gurley.

should add commercial pH-lowering solutions, peat moss, oak leaves, limbs, driftwood, and even "blackwater" solutions to keep them healthy long-term. These species include Matamatas (*Chelus fimbriatus*), Amazon River Turtles (*Podocnemis* species), Twist-necked Turtles *(Platemys)*, Spiny-necked Turtles *(Acanthochelys)*, Snake-necked Turtles *(Hydromedusa)*, and many of the *Phrynops* and *Batrachemys* species.

Water Temperature

Water temperature is important. Like other reptiles, environmental temperature is important for behavior and for proper digestion of food in turtles. Those species from tropical environments will tend to stop eating and become inactive when kept too cold. This stress can lead to health issues such as respiratory infections. Those species inhabiting cool mountain streams do poorly when kept in warm captive environments with still water. Obviously your goal is to research a species' natural habitat and special requirements and decide if you can meet its needs before you purchase any animals. **It is important to remember that for most species, room temperature is too cold.**

Water can be warmed in a variety of ways. Many keepers use submersible aquarium heaters within their enclosures. There are a variety of brands and styles available. We suggest that you invest in a high-quality, durable heater such as Ebo Jäger® or a titanium heater. It is our experience that the inexpensive models tend to break easily, burn out, or even worse, have faulty thermostats that dangerously overheat the water in the enclosure without warning.

We have found that small reptile heating pads can work great for warming the water in small enclosures. We place one under one end of the enclosure and keep it on the low setting. The temperature should be carefully monitored for a couple of days before adding any turtles to make sure the recommended range of temperatures is safely achieved. Benefits of heating pads include the fact that the equipment is located on the outside of the enclosure.

Water Changes

Many keepers simply drain and refill their turtle's indoor enclosure weekly, twice a month, or monthly, depending on the system that the keeper has established. This method is easy for the keeper and guarantees that the water is cleaned without the use of expensive filters. Some keepers refill the tubs with water that has already been filtered, warmed, and is chlorine-free. Their feeling is that the disturbance of running a water hose into an enclosure is somewhat stressful for the turtles, and a flood of cold, chlorinated water from a hose can cause problems. Most turtles, especially those that are well-acclimated, apparently weather this flurry of activity and disturbance quite well. For more sensitive species, we suggest a calmer method of cleaning and changing the water such as gently adding prepared water to the enclosure.

The Filter

In small enclosures such as aquariums, we add an external filter or a sponge filter to keep the water clean and aerated. Filtration helps in several ways - Excessive waste in the water from overcrowding or poor filtration adds ammonia to the system, which can raise the pH of the water. In addition to smelling horrible, harmful bacteria can grow rapidly and ruin the "health" of your turtle enclosure. Such water will allow even minor injuries to become life-threatening, causing eye irritation, non-healing sores, shell rot, and other health problems.

An inexpensive external filter will work well to keep the water in your turtle's enclosure clean and aerated.

Heat and Lighting

A small, low wattage (40-watt or 60-watt) heat lamp in a clamp-type fixture should be placed above the land area of an aquatic turtle's enclosure. This area will serve as the basking site, the area where the turtle will dry out and absorb heat (and beneficial UVB rays from an additional source). The extended length of a 20-gallon long aquarium (30"*l* x 12"*w* x 12"*h*) keeps turtles from overheating by allowing them an end that is warm under the basking lamp, but allows them the other end to get out of the heat. UVB-emitting bulbs should be mounted overhead in a shop light fixture or aquarium light fixture.

With a little work and creativity, indoor enclosures can closely approximate the natural environment of the turtles living within. Photo by Russ Gurley.

Some keepers choose to add a low-watt submersible aquarium heater to add additional warmth to the system. In any event, your goal for most species is a water temperature of 76° to 82° F (24° to 27° C) and a basking spot in the 90° to 95° F (32° to 35° C) range. Again, getting the enclosure ready early allows you to establish the basking spot, to set up a good filter, to set the water temperature, and to establish water quality.

The North American Wood Turtle, *Actinemys insculpta*, is one of the hardiest of the semi-aquatic species being produced by turtle breeders. Photo by Russ Gurley.

Semi-Aquatic and Terrestrial Species

The Enclosure

Most box turtles, many leaf turtles, North American Wood Turtles, Spotted Turtles, and other more terrestrial species can also spend their early days in a glass aquarium or small tub. Again, the length of a 20-gallon long aquarium helps the keeper maintain a temperature gradient within the enclosure with a warm end and a cooler end.

The Water

Make sure that small semi-aquatic and terrestrial turtles can climb in and out of their water source easily. Keep the water level lower (½" to 1") for the more water-loving species. Use a 1-2" layer of a damp peat and sand mixture with sphagnum moss on top for the more terrestrial species. For both turtles that enjoy damper conditions and those that enjoy drier environments,

This forest floor type enclosure is ideal for small wood turtles, spotted turtles, box turtles, and other forest-dwelling species. Photo by Russ Gurley.

maintain a a basking area. The substrate for semi-aquatic species can range from paper towel to a sand-peat mix, cypress mulch, soil, or even commercially available reptile carpet. Here also a heating pad underneath can help maintain the desired warmth of the enclosure. This heat beneath the water section or damp land area will also keep the overall humidity of the enclosure high.

We typically offer water to young semi-aquatic and terrestrial species in a flat dish such as a petrie dish,

This large semi-aquatic enclosure is home to a group of Twist-necked Turtles (*Platemys platycephala*). Photo by Russ Gurley.

plant saucer, or paint tray. (The paint tray is sloped and provides easy access into and out of the water for smaller turtles.) The water container should be depressed slightly into the substrate to give smaller turtles easy access to the water.

Heat and Lighting

In a terrestrial setup, heat can be provided by an incandescent bulb (40-watt to 100-watt) in a clamp-type fixture mounted above the enclosure or by a heating pad underneath the enclosure, depending on the requirements of the individual species.

T-Rex UVB-heat® bulbs in clamp fixtures provide both heat and UVB while ZooMed 7.0® UVB-emitting bulbs in shop light fixtures provide UVB without the production of heat. Both are excellent to put over a turtle's enclosure. These high-quality UVB-emitting bulbs should be placed above all turtles and tortoises, especially young turtles that are eating a lot and growing rapidly.

Keeping Turtles Outside

As sun worshipers, turtles reap the benefits of being kept outside in direct sunlight. However, you must be careful to

This simple outdoor enclosure created from landscaping lumber provides an excellent home for terrestrial turtles and/or tortoises. Photo by Russ Gurley.

protect your turtles from predators when you are keeping them outside.

Cement-mixing tubs are fine enclosures for small turtles. They are inexpensive and easy to clean. Photo by Russ Gurley.

Raccoons, opossums, foxes, dogs and cats are all likely turtle predators. Be mindful of animals that you do not normally consider predators, including birds and ants. Both are known to eat small turtles in the wild and to eat plenty of turtles in outside captive pens as well.

Aquatic turtles do very well in outside pens or pools. Be careful –

This home-made bog is home to a large breeding group of Spotted Turtles (*Clemmys guttata*). Courtesy of Wayne Hill. Photo by Russ Gurley.

young turtles are masters of disappearing into their surroundings. They will disappear quickly by either digging or hiding in foliage. It's what they do.

Add some interesting plants to your turtle enclosures. Strawberries, blackberries, cantaloupe, and other fruits and vegetables make great additions. They will not only provide cover and some food, they will attract insects that will add variety to their diet. As your young turtle grows, feed it a balanced and

Large stock tanks are available at agricultural stores. They can be easily converted into interesting homes for turtles. Courtesy of Marc Cantos. Photo by Russ Gurley.

varied diet. Your goal is to produce a vigorous, alert adult that will live a long, healthy life in your care.

Large swimming pools can be set up outdoors for turtles. They provide a lot of water for keeping larger species or breeding groups of smaller turtles. Courtesy of Wayne Hill. Photo by Russ Gurley.

Chapter THREE: **Feeding**

An Eastern Box Turtle, *Terrapene carolina carolina*, enjoys an afternoon snack of a bright red tomato. Photo by Russ Gurley.

As your turtles grow, continue to offer them a wide variety of food. Do not overfeed your turtle. Keep in mind that a baby's stomach is roughly the size of its eye. The key is quality and diversity rather than quantity. Your goal is to see slow, physically correct growth without signs of obesity, shell deformities, and other nutrition-related problems. It is so exciting to watch a baby turtle slowly grow into a healthy and beautiful juvenile, sub-adult, and adult.

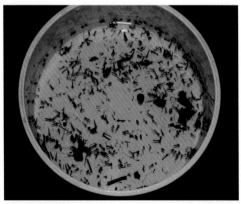

Mosquito larvae are very attractive prey items for most small turtles. Photo by Russ Gurley.

Turtles require a diet that may include commercial pelleted food, fruits and vegetables, small mice, redworms and earthworms. Photo by Russ Gurley.

Feeding Aquatic Species

Turtles should be fed a wide variety of foods. We have found that most small aquatic turtles eagerly feed on small guppies and mosquito larvae. They will also typically be excited to feed on live invertebrates such as redworms, blackworms, mealworms, and small crickets. Once the turtle begins feeding well, add a few small commercial pellets to its diet. In many cases, baby turtles often do not follow the feeding patterns of adults. Typically, most freshwater turtle species will begin life with an insectivorous diet. Only a few species will be eager to eat fruit and vegetable matter as babies. These include Amazon river turtles, map turtles, Central and South American wood turtles, North American wood turtles, and a handful of others. Great first foods for these herbivores include live aquatic plants, finely grated greens and vegetables, and small amounts of banana, watermelon, strawberries, and cantaloupe. Remember: Healthy growth and good nutrition are so important in these early stages.

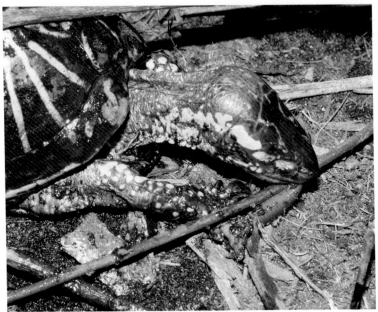
Many species, such as this Florida Box Turtle (*Terrapene carolina bauri*), will enjoy earthworms as part of their varied diet. Photo by Russ Gurley.

Feeding Semi-Aquatic and Terrestrial Species

There will also be variety in the feeding patterns of terrestrial species. Some will prefer to eat in the water and some will prefer to eat on land. Most freshwater turtle species, even those that are largely herbivorous as adults, begin life as insectivores, feeding on a wide variety of insects and insect larvae. Experiment if the lifestyle and dietary needs of your turtle is not apparent right away. Small redworms, blackworms, and wax worms can be placed in a shallow dish such as a petrie dish or small jar lid. Small crickets can be dropped into the enclosure every few days. All of these invertebrates should be dusted with vitamin powder and a high-quality calcium supplement every few feedings as the young turtles grow. We mix calcium with Vitamin D3 and a high-quality multivitamin powder in a 2:1 ratio. This added vitamin and calcium supplementation assures your turtle will grow in a healthy manner.

Food for Your Turtles

Carnivorous Species
Most carnivorous species will require a diet that contains some live prey. We suggest a quality mix of commercial turtle food and the addition of a variety of live prey including:

Earthworms   Redworms   Blackworms   Wax worms
Mosquito larvae   Guppies * Can be offered in a dish or in the shallow aquatic end of an enclosure.

Herbivorous Species
Strict herbivores are rare, but those kept feed on a variety of greens and other vegetables and an assortment of fruit. Most herbivores will eat commercial turtle diets, but a keeper should be cautious to not overfeed as most diets are high in protein and fats. We suggest these foods for herbivorous species:

Commercial turtle food (low fat / low protein)   Romaine lettuce
Kale   Carrot tops   Red cabbage   Zucchini   Yellow Squash
Sweet Potato   Mixed Veggies   Banana   Mango
Cantaloupe   Watermelon   Apple   Pear   Grapes (split)
Strawberries

The Spiny Turtle, *Heosemys spinosa*, will enjoy salads consisting of mixed fruit and vegetables as babies and adults. Photo by Bill Love.

The Giant Leaf Turtle, *Heosemys grandis*, is an eager feeder on a wide range of items including mice, worms, and fruits and vegetables. Photo by Russ Gurley.

Omnivorous Species

Omnivores will eat a variety of food items. We typically feed our omnivores the "meat" portion of their diets (earthworms, fish, mice, and commercial turtle food) two to three times a week. They are also fed a salad consisting of chopped greens, shredded vegetables, and fruit (depending on that species' needs) once or twice a week. Their menu includes:

Commercial turtle food   Earthworms   Redworms
Blackworms   Wax worms   Mosquito larvae   Mice
Guppies or small fish   Banana   Cantaloupe   Grapes (split)
Strawberries   Red bell peppers   Dandelions   Grated or finely sliced Mixed Vegetables

Chapter FOUR: **Health**

Treating small turtles can be very tedious and stressful for the turtles. Extreme care must be taken. Photo by Russ Gurley.

Periodically, a turtle keeper should pull a turtle out of its environment and check it for signs of health-related problems. The turtle should be checked for signs of respiratory problems or nutritional deficiencies as these are two of the most common causes of death in captive turtles.

Respiratory Problems

Respiratory problems are typically caused when turtles are chilled by a sudden drop in temperature combined with poor captive conditions and stress. A gaping mouth or bubbling nostrils are signs of respiratory problems. Also, aquatic species with respiratory issues will tend to tilt to one side while swimming or will be unable to submerge completely. Minor respiratory problems can often be corrected by the addition of heat to the environment. Moderate to severe cases will require a routine of antibiotics administered by a qualified veterinarian We suggest that keepers find a qualified reptile veterinarian <u>before</u> they experience problems.

The Association of Reptile and Amphibian Veterinarians (A.R.A.V.) is an organization that can help you find a veterinarian in your area. The A.R.A.V. is a non-profit international organization of veterinarians and herpetologists founded in 1991. Their goal is to improve reptilian and amphibian veterinary care and husbandry through education, exchange of ideas, and research. The Association of Reptilian and Amphibian Veterinarians (A.R.A.V.) promotes conservation and humane treatment of all reptilian and amphibian species through education, captive breeding, and habitat preservation. Check out www.arav.org for more information.

Eyes and Mouths

Bright, energetic eyes are signs of a healthy turtle. Dull, hazy eyes are signs of potential problems. Among the most common causes of eye-related problems are respiratory-related illnesses, poor water quality, and improper diet.

Partially closed, puffy, and runny eyes (usually combined with a nasal discharge) are generally signs of a respiratory infection. If caught early and treated with the proper antibiotics, turtles will generally improve quite quickly. Occasionally, closed puffy eyes are signs of a nutritional deficiency (lack of vitamin A).

A turtle's mouth should be smooth, clean, and held tightly closed. Missing tissue, asymmetry, lumps, or bleeding can be signs of injury.

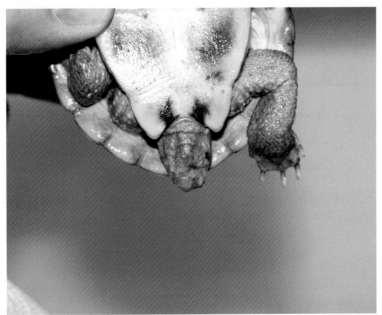

When turtles are crowded or when more than one male turtle are kept together, serious biting injuries can occur. Photo by Russ Gurley.

Injuries

If kept together, especially in a crowded situation, turtles can be aggressive and may bite each other's legs, heads, or tails. Check these areas for signs of injury. Minor injuries can usually be cleaned up with warm water and the application of an antibiotic cream such as Silvadene® or a triple antibiotic ointment such as Neosporin®. More serious injuries may necessitate a visit to a veterinarian, especially if stitches are required.

If biting injuries occur, it is time to evaluate your turtle setup. Your turtles might be too cramped or you might need to feed the turtles a little more. Perhaps you can add cage decorations such as additional basking spots and places for the turtles to separate themselves from each other. Be curious and attentive. When you discover the problem, change the situation that is causing the problem.

Lumps or assymetry to the head are common signs of an ear infection. Turtles with these symptoms should be seen by a qualified veterinarian as soon as possible. Photo by Russ Gurley.

Occasionally, aggressive cagemates will attack an animal that is weakened. If this is the case, the turtle should be set up in an enclosure by itself while it recovers.

Betadine®

A gentle scrub with Betadine® is felt by most turtle veterinarians to be the best treatment for most shell and skin infections.

Swelling

Check all feet for swelling. Swelling is usually a symptom of an injury, an infection, or in some cases (wild-caught animals), the presence of a renal parasite. Minor sores will usually heal on their own if the turtle is isolated from other turtles and is kept in clean, aerated water and has access to a dry, well-heated basking spot. Adding aquarium salt or Epsom salt to the water (one tablespoon per gallon) can help in the healing process. We suggest you consult a veterinarian for any swelling, especially irregularities around the head of the turtle.

Ear infections are common in some species (sliders, map turtles, box turtles, etc.), especially when they are kept in enclosures with poor water quality or in other unhygienic conditions. Affected turtles will usually show a moderate to severe swelling on one side or both sides of the head. These swellings are typically abscesses that will need to be lanced and drained. This is a procedure best carried out by a qualified veterinarian.

Open Wounds and Sores

To treat a small open wound or sore, dry the injured area with a towel. Clean the area with warm water and place Silvadene® cream or a triple antibiotic ointment such as Neosporin® on the sore. Keep the turtle dry on a clean substrate in a box or secure container for several hours. Return the patient to an enclosure with plenty of fresh water and a hot basking spot (90° to 95° F for

Mild cases of shell rot can be treated successfully. This Spiny-necked Turtle, *Acanthochelys spixii*, will rest for a couple of hours with a coating of Silvadene® before being placed back into its enclosure. Photo by Russ Gurley.

most species). Continue the treatment once a day for several days, always returning the turtle to an enclosure with clean, aerated water and plenty of heat and sunshine whenever possible. The addition of several tablespoons of aquarium or sea salt per gallon of water can help in the healing process. For more serious wounds, see a veterinarian.

Shell Rot

Signs of shell rot include pitting of the shell, sores on the shell, and in extreme cases, damage to or loss of the coverings to the scutes. Most cases of shell rot arise from the combination of an injury and abnormal bacterial growth in poor water conditions. Shell flaking, bleeding, and loss of scutes are signs of more severe shell rot. Mild cases can be treated with a Betadine® scrub and application of Silvadene® cream or Acriflavin® (as a swab or dip). More severe cases may require a round of injectable (parenteral) antibiotic treatments in addition to the Betadine® scrubs. Baytril® (Enrofloxacine) has proven to be an effective treatment for some of the more severe cases of shell rot.

Septicemia

Septicemia is a generalized systemic infection. Septicemia is sometimes caused by gram-negative bacteria entering the body through a cut or sore. It is very dangerous and should be caught in the early stages to be treated effectively. Characteristics of septicemia in turtles include an unusual pinkish or reddish tint to legs and other soft tissue (and the plastron), and splotchy redness on the tongue and insides of the mouth. This redness is caused by local (petechial or echymotic) hemorrhaging.

Tail and Vent

Some more aggressive turtle species will bite each other's tails, especially if several specimens are kept in a small enclosure. Check for injuries and clean any with clean water and antibiotic ointment if necessary. Young turtles, probably from a strong feeding response, will bite their cagemates' tails. These nub tails will usually heal quickly if the water is clean.

Salmonellosis

Turtles and *Salmonella*

During the early 1970s, small pet turtles, mostly Red-eared Sliders and map turtles were kept as pets in an estimated 4% of all U.S. homes. During the 1960s and early 1970s an estimated 280,000 infants and small children were diagnosed as having turtle-associated Salmonellosis (Gersden, S. 1994). Most of these cases were small children who had placed the turtles in their mouths or handled the turtles and then placed their fingers in their mouths. In 1975, as a result of these incidences, the U.S. Food and Drug Administration prohibited the distribution and sale of turtles with a shell length of four inches or less.

As mentioned, there has been a tremendous awareness lately in the needs of captive turtles. Breeders are producing more baby turtles than ever before. As turtles and tortoises become more popular as pets, some concerns over Salmonellosis infections continue to pop up.

Most people today know that *Salmonella* bacteria are also commonly found in beef, chicken, chicken eggs, and some types of *Salmonella* are even endemic in human populations in parts of the world. There is nonetheless the real possibility of small children and immuno-compromised people becoming infected by turtles if their turtles are kept in unclean conditions and if they do not follow common sense sanitary procedures when working with their animals.

* <u>Recommendations for Preventing Transmission of *Salmonella* from Reptiles to Humans</u>

1. Persons at increased risk for infection or serious complications of Salmonellosis (e.g., pregnant women, children younger than five years, and immuno-compromised persons such as persons with AIDS) should avoid contact with reptiles.

2. Reptiles should not be kept in child-care centers and may not be appropriate pets in households in which persons at increased risk for infection reside.

3. Veterinarians and pet store owners should provide information to potential purchasers and owners of reptiles about the increased risk of acquiring Salmonellosis from reptiles.

4. Veterinarians and operators of pet stores should advise reptile owners always to wash their hands after handling reptiles and reptile cages.

5. To prevent contamination of food-preparation areas (e.g., kitchens) and other selected sites, reptiles should be kept out of these areas - in particular, kitchen sinks should not be used to bathe reptiles or to wash reptile dishes, cages, or aquariums.

From Texas Agricultural Extension Service Newsletter, Texas A&M University System, Volume 11, Number 3, July-September 1995.

Fungal Infections

Fungal infections, characterized by gray (or whitish) fuzzy patches on the shell or skin of a turtle can be signs of too much dead matter in the turtle's enclosure. Fungus lives and multiplies in the leaves, uneaten food, and fecal material that settle in the bottom of a turtle's home. Fungus commonly arrives on sick feeder fish, especially goldfish, that have been kept in unsanitary conditions. Fungal infections are usually associated with an injury and often need an injury or a shell scrape on which to anchor.

Fungal infections should be treated with a scrub of Betadine®, Acriflavine, Silvadene®, or a triple antibiotic lotion such as Neosporin®.

Salt

Many marsh-dwelling species, especially Diamondback Terrapins and many of the soft-shelled turtles, are found in brackish water in nature. Therefore, the addition of non-iodized aquarium salt or sea salt (from one tablespoon to four tablespoons per gallon, depending on the species) can be beneficial in keeping them healthy. A saline environment inhibits the growth of fungus and certain bacteria.

NUTRITIONAL CONCERNS / Vitamin Deficiencies

If a baby turtle shows symptoms of nutritional problems and is still feeding, switch to a high-quality diet with the addition of a variety of the best commercial foods, healthy live insects, fruits, and vegetables (according to the species feeding habits). Some keepers will even inject vitamins into a fish, banana, or other favorite food. Vitamin powder can be sprinkled onto most food items given to semi-aquatic and terrestrial species quite easily.

Calcium Deficiency

Metabolic bone disease is a major cause of death in captive hatchling turtles (Highfield, 1996). An early warning sign of MBD is a soft plastron (lower shell) or a carapace (top shell) that feels soft to the touch. By offering foods rich in calcium (romaine lettuce, kale, broccoli, carrot tops, water lettuce, water hyacinth, watercress, etc.) and by adding sprinkles of high-quality calcium supplements to food, this disfiguring and fatal condition can be prevented and even turned around if caught in the early stages.

For aquatic carnivores, most commercial pellets will have ample calcium to prevent problems. If the turtles are also eating fish, insects, and other live prey, they will gain calcium from these sources as well. For those species that feed on land, calcium and Vitamin D3 supplements should be sprinkled over dishes of earthworms, shaken onto crickets, or added to their favorite salad. In addition, many omnivorous species will eat some calcium-containing greens in their diet. Be mindful to add greens that are high in calcium such as dark green lettuce, kale, carrot tops, and others. Many aquatic species may be tempted more by "wild" plants such as water lettuce, water hyacinth, watercress, and duckweed.

Calcium deficiency is rarely seen in herbivorous species that are fed a wide variety of plant matter. Turtles that are fed incorrect food items such as dog or cat food or ones that are fed solely on a commercial turtle diet are the most likely to experience calcium deficiencies. Aquatic herbivores can be fed low protein / low fat pelleted food in addition to the aquatic vegetation that is high in calcium.

Vitamin D3 Deficiency

This condition usually develops from a lack of sunlight in captive conditions. Its symptoms include swollen mouths and limbs and lethargy. By giving specimens access to plenty of sunlight and by adding fluorescent fixtures with high-quality UVB-emitting bulbs over their indoor enclosures, this condition can be curtailed before it develops. By adding a vitamin powder that is rich in D3, this problem can be avoided. For aquatic species, choose commercial feeds that contain plenty of calcium and Vitamin D3 or add powder containing Vitamin D3 to dampened pellets or onto foods that are eaten on land. For semi-aquatic and terrestrial species, add Vitamin D3 to their food following the manufacturer's recommendations. Try to place turtles in direct sunlight as much as possible.

Vitamin A Deficiency

In aquatic species, this condition is usually dietary. Its symptoms can include swollen eyes, sores on the skin, and respiratory problems. The addition of aquatic plants, greens, and other veggies, especially carrots, to a turtle's diet, can help prevent this problem before it develops. Keepers should carefully research the needs of the species they keep and investigate the nutritional contents of the commercial food they are offering to make sure the proper ingredients are contained. Most commercial diets have the proper basic ingredients to maintain a healthy turtle, especially for the carnivorous species. Mild cases of Vitamin A deficiency can be corrected with 1-2 drops of cod liver oil added to a turtle's meal. In extreme cases, Vitamin A injections can be administered. A keeper must be observant, as a Vitamin A overdose closely resembles a Vitamin A deficiency. Having a single veterinarian that treats your collection can help avoid the problem of too much intervention.

Vitamin E Deficiency

This condition develops when keepers feed a diet that is almost exclusively fish and high fat foods to their captive turtles. In fact, some commercial feeds cause deficiency of all fat soluble vitamins – A, E, and D (McCord, pers. com.). The main manifestations of deficiencies of these vitamins are in reproductive problems and the production of infertile eggs. It is especially common in herbivorous species being fed an improper high fat diet and those being fed lots of thawed frozen fish. (The freezing process removes most or all of the Vitamin E normally found in fish.) Vitamin E deficiency can be avoided by feeding turtles a wide variety of foods, including food items that are lower in fat and protein (apples, peaches, pumpkin, chard, dandelion greens, etc.).

Poisoning

In outdoor enclosures, overlying trees and nearby plants often shed leaves and flowers into the turtles' enclosure. Turtles will usually eat this vegetation. If any of this foliage is toxic, problems including paralysis and drowning can occur.

* SOME COMMON POISONOUS PLANTS

Avocado (leaves)	Carnation
Bird of Paradise	Chinese Lantern
Bottlebrush	Christmas Cactus
Caladium	Chrysanthemum
Calla Lilly	Clematis

Common Privet
Cone Flower
Daisy
Day Lily
Dieffenbachia
Dogwood
Dracaena
English Ivy
Eucalyptus
Foxglove
Hemlock
Impatiens
Iris
Ivy
Jasmine
Larkspur
Lily of the Valley
Mesquite
Milk Weed
Mistletoe
Morning Glory
Mushrooms
    (some wild species)
Nandina
Oak
Oleander
Peach (leaves, pit)
Peony
Periwinkle
Philodendron
Poinsettia
Poison Ivy
Poison Oak
Poison Sumac
Pokeweed
Potato (leaves)
Pothos Ivy
Privet
Rhododendron
Rhubarb
Sage
Sago Palm
Schefflera
Snapdragon
Sweet Pea
Sweet Potato
Tomato (leaves)
Tulip
Verbena
Vinca
Walnut hulls
Wisteria
Yew
Yucca

* This list was compiled from conversations with various turtle and tortoise keepers, from the reference below, and from personal experience. A very good list is available from the California Turtle and Tortoise Club's Poisonous Plant List printed in the **Tortuga Gazette 28(1): 8-10, January 1992** and found on their website at **www.tortoise.org**. Their list is based on the University of California Irvine's Regional Poison Center list of plants that are toxic or potentially toxic to humans.

Turtles occasionally drown each other. Here, a larger male Wood Turtle (*Clemmys insculpta*) holds another male under the water in a misguided mating attempt. Photo by Russ Gurley.

Drowning

Believe it or not, having an aquatic turtle drown is not a completely unusual occurrence. In most cases, a turtle will get trapped underwater in the opening of a concrete block or under a piece of decoration, or other structure. Another common way a turtle drowns is that it gets too cold during a surprise cold day and becomes so lethargic that it sinks to the bottom of the pond.

If you find a turtle that has drowned, do not immediately assume that it is dead. Quickly remove the turtle from the water and hold it upside-down until the water stops dripping from its nose. You can gently swing the turtle back and forth to remove as much water from its lungs as possible. Then, set the turtle on

Enclosures that provide turtles with clean water, proper heat and lighting, and excellent shelters will keep stress related to captivity to a minimum. This a secretive pair of Pan's Box Turtles, *Cuora pani*. Photo by Russ Gurley.

the ground or a tabletop with its head fully extended and push the front legs slowly in and out. I wouldn't try mouth-to-mouth – see Salmonellosis in this chapter.

If you have a veterinarian nearby that has reptile experience, take the turtle there quickly. There are respiratory stimulants that can be administered. If the turtle recovers, we suggest keeping it at room temperature, alone, and quiet for the following month and a round of antibiotics should be administered during this time.

Obesity

In captivity, many keepers overfeed their turtles. An obese turtle is recognized by the fat hanging out behind the legs, around the head, and by the tail. This unhealthy condition can be avoided by keeping your turtle in a creative environment that is not cramped and by not feeding it too much. We suggest feeding baby turtles a varied diet of small meals every other day. Obese captive animals often experience liver and kidney problems related to fat storage in their bodies. This condition will greatly shorten the life of your turtle.

Stress

As with many animals, stress does not exhibit a definite set of characteristics in turtles and tortoises. In fact, stress manifests itself in a variety of ways in captive turtles. Luckily, most captive-hatched turtles seem to show very few symptoms of stress. Many appear to be quite tame and even inquisitive, especially at dinner time.

HOW TO AVOID STRESS IN CAPTIVE TURTLES

1. Provide your turtles with enough space. Access to sunlight and fresh water with qualities consistent with their natural habitat, live plants, and naturalistic decorations provide the best captive conditions for your turtles.

2. A wide variety of food, both natural and commercial, keeps stress to a minimum.

3. Many turtle species are solitary in the wild. Keeping multiple animals, especially multiple males in a single enclosure, can be a situation that stresses some specimens, especially smaller, subordinate males. However, in some cases, keeping multiple males in an enclosure during breeding season seems to stimulate dominant males to breed with females. Use your judgment. Having a couple of extra enclosures for shuffling turtles around is always a nice luxury.

Hibernation of Young Turtles

Most keepers choose not to let young turtles hibernate until they are two or three years old. Young turtles from temperate areas and that are healthy and heavy are easier to hibernate. Hibernating turtles are typically placed in a 'hibernation box' in a secure closet, garage, or outdoor shed where a deep freeze is unlikely to cause the animals to get too cold and where they can

An enclosure that provides clean water, a secure shelter, and the necessary environmental temperatures will be the main component to minimizing stress in captive turtles. Photo by Russ Gurley.

be monitored. Prior to hibernation, turtles are given access to water but are not fed for one to two weeks to allow all waste to be removed from their systems. After this time, they must have good weight and have an overall healthy appearance to be hibernated. The 'hibernation box' is a large plastic tub that is usually filled with a slightly damp mixture of potting soil, topsoil, and leaf mulch and with grass clippings or hay placed on top. The turtles are given access to water, but are not fed during this time of dormancy. After the hibernation period of one to three months, the turtles are warmed gradually (over a two-week period) from their hibernating temperature of 50° to 55° F (10° to 13° C) to a 'springtime' temperature of 75° to 85° F (24° to 29° C). They are then fed a varied diet to prepare them for healthy growth during the spring and summer. During this time, those turtles that feed on land should receive an extra sprinkle or two of calcium powder added to their food every few feedings.

We suggest that you move your young turtles outside as soon as possible during the spring. Natural sunlight is very beneficial

Outdoor enclosures should offer turtles plenty of shelter from the heat and from potential predators. Photo by Russ Gurley.

to healthy growth. Be careful that you don't move young turtles into a situation where they can overheat. Glass aquariums "trap" heat and can heat up to dangerous temperatures very quickly. They should not be used outside.

The Future

We hope that the days of turtles as disposable pets are long behind us. Keeping your turtle healthy, active, and alert will give you pride in your husbandry skills with these wonderful reptile pets. As your turtle thrives and grows, you may want to expand your collection. Many turtle keepers are deciding to specialize in a certain species or a specific group of turtles after they become confident in their skills. One goal for many keepers is to establish pairs of turtles and to breed them. As a successful turtle breeder, you will be able to offer new keepers your healthy offspring to spark their adventure into this wonderful area of herpetoculture. If you hope to expand your work with a certain species, you will probably want to trade some of your turtles for turtles from another breeder. Enhanced genetic diversity of all captive populations of reptiles should be one of our non-wavering goals. Keep good records. Share all relevant information with those who purchase turtles from you or to other breeders with whom you trade animals.

As wild turtles receive pressure from a variety of sources, the growing captive population of turtles becomes more and more important for the future of many species. Also, as the population of turtle keepers who can successfully raise a turtle to adulthood increases, this group and their skills will become very important in the fight to save the world's threatened species.

INDIVIDUAL SPECIES ACCOUNTS

Even small hatchling Red-eared Sliders will thrive under proper care. This is a pastel Red-eared Slider. Photo by Russ Gurley.

The **Red-eared Slider** (*Trachemys scripta elegans*) is surely one of the world's hardiest and most prolific turtles. It is an omnivore, feeding on a wide variety of food with adults being mostly herbivorous. Young turtles should be fed a mixture of the best commercial diets and also small worms, crickets, and even feeder guppies. These turtles grow quite large with females reaching 15" to 18" and males typically much smaller.

The **Florida Red-bellied Turtle** (*Pseudemys nelsoni*) is a warmth-loving species found throughout the Everglades in nature. As would be expected, it requires warm, clean water. This species is omnivorous. Females grow to 16" and males reach 10".

Painted Turtles (*Chrysemys* species) are the smallest and possibly the most attractive of North America's painted turtles.

The Southern Painted Turtle (*Chrysemys picta dorsalis*) is one of the most beautiful North American turtles. Photo by Russ Gurley.

They feed on commercial turtle food, insects, small fish, and plant matter. Warm, filtered water and at least one sturdy basking area should be offered.

Chicken turtles (*Deirochelys reticularia*) have an adoring following among turtle enthusiasts. They are a medium-sized turtle (to 10") that are avid baskers and will spend time on land. Young of this species feed on aquatic insects and other invertebrates and become more herbivorous with age.

Map turtles (*Graptemys* species) require warm, aerated water to simulate

The Southern Black-knobbed Map Turtle (*G. n. delticola*) is one of the rarest North American species in captive breeding programs. Photo by Russ Gurley.

Graptemys flavimaculata, the Yellow-blotched Map Turtle is listed as an endangered species even though it is being produced in some numbers in breeding programs. Photo by Russ Gurley.

their flowing river homes. They feed on a variety of animal and plant matter and the babies love mosquito larvae and blackworms in addition to a high-quality commercial turtle food. Most map turtles are highly sexually dimorphic with adult females reaching 10" to 12" and most males maturing at only 4".

The **Common Snapping Turtle** (*Chelydra serpentina*) makes a wonderful pet turtle because it is hardy and feeds very well on a wide variety of food. Food should include earthworms, redworms, crickets, small

A young Common Snapping Turtle. Photo by Russ Gurley.

fish, and a mixture of high-quality commercial turtle food. They do get quite large (18") and can become aggressive even when raised in captivity. They are best kept individually in creative enclosures with live plants and a variety of underwater decorations such as branches, leaves, and driftwood.

The worm-like lure at the tip of the tongue is seen in this awesome Alligator Snapping Turtle. Photo by Kurt Edwards.

The **Alligator Snapping Turtle** (*Macrochelys temminckii*) can be a wonderful pet when obtained as a captive-produced animal. They are somewhat shy and secretive and babies will stop eating if handled too much. They thrive on a diet of live fish and invertebrates and when kept in a large enclosure that offers warm (78° to 82° F), clean, low pH water. Adult males can reach 150 pounds and lengths of 30". Adult females are smaller, typically in the 40 pound and 14" range.

Mud and Musk Turtles (*Kinosternon* and *Sternotherus* species) are wonderful small turtles that make great pets. They are alert and inquisitive and most specimens stay small (4" to 7"). They eat a variety of food and thrive in clean, filtered water. Offer them plenty of underwater decorations such as driftwood,

bark, and stone piles to explore and add live plants to help keep their environment healthy.

The Three-striped Mud Turtle, *Kinosternon bauri*, is a hardy species found throughout the southeastern United States. Photo by Russ Gurley.

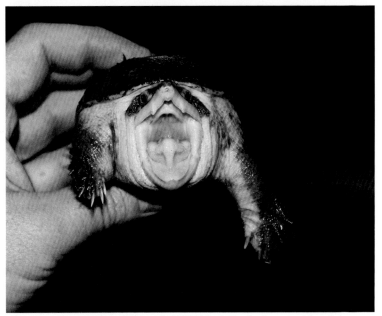

Claudius angustatus, the Narrow-bridged Musk Turtle, is an exciting (but aggressive) species that is unfortunately rare in captive breeding programs. Photo by Russ Gurley.

Giant Musk Turtles (*Staurotypus triporcatus*) are the largest of the musk turtles. They are hardy when offered large enclosures with clean warm water. They will feed aggressively on fish, mice, and commercial turtle foods. Care must be taken that they are not overfed and they are given plenty of room for

exercise as they can become dangerously obese. Also, Giant Musk Turtles feed on smaller turtles in nature and they will do so in your aquarium. It is best not to mix them with other turtles.

Giant Musk Turtles start out life small. They are, however, very hardy and quickly grow into large beasts. Courtesy of Wayne Hill. Photo by Russ Gurley.

Captive-hatched Diamondback Terrapins, unlike wild-caught specimens, typically thrive in captivity. Photo by Russ Gurley.

Diamondback Terrapins (*Malaclemys terrapin*) are being kept and bred in ever-increasing numbers in the United States. They thrive on a captive diet of commercial pellets with the addition of fish and redworms. Dried shrimp and krill are a great treat for these turtles. They require warm (74° to 78° F) clean water and many keepers add one tablespoon of aquarium salt per gallon of water into their diamondback enclosures as this species is found in coastal saline environments in nature.

Soft-shelled Turtles (*Apalone*, *Aspideretes*, *Trionyx*, *Chitra*, and *Pelochelys* species) require a dedicated keeper and are typically not for beginners. In general these turtles require heavily filtered and aerated water with a thick sandy substrate and the addition of driftwood and live plants. Water temperature needs vary from warm for specimens from the southeastern United States to cooler for the larger species that live in the deep rivers of the world.

Soft-shelled turtles are carnivorous, feeding on a variety of invertebrate prey and live fish. Most will take the additional meal of a high-quality commercial turtle food

Small Spiny Soft-shells, *Apalone spinifera*, will spend time on a sandy basking area under UVB and heat-emitting lamps. Photo by Russ Gurley.

once or twice a week. Most species are aggressive, will bite readily, and can reach lengths of 12" to 16". *Apalone ferox*, the Florida Soft-shelled Turtle, reaches an adult length of over 20". The larger species such as *Pelochelys* and *Chitra* are typically very aggressive and can grow to lengths of over 36". They will

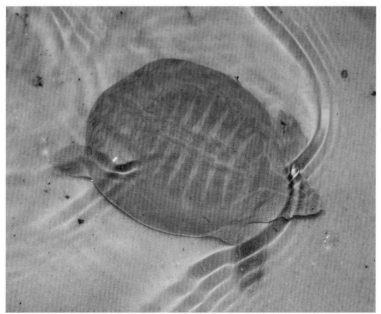

The needs of *Chitra indica*, the Asian Giant Soft-shelled Turtle, far exceed what most turtle keepers can meet. It requires clean, cool water, a deep sand substrate, live prey, and a very large enclosure as it can reach 40" in total length. Photo by Russ Gurley.

obviously require enclosures that are far larger than most keepers can maintain.

European Pond Turtles (*Emys orbicularis*) are hardy little turtles (8") that thrive in a clean aquatic environment. They enjoy commercial turtle diets with the addition of redworms, blackworms, and small fish. As they grow, they will eat more plant material so aquatic plants and greens should be added to their diets.

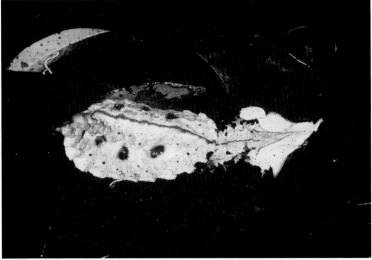

This small Matamata will require water that is acidic and soft to survive well long-term. It will benefit from live plants and plenty of shelters in its enclosure. Photo by Bill Love.

The **Matamata** (*Chelus fimbriatus*) is an Amazon River native and is surely one of the world's most unusual turtles. They are masters of disguise and sit quietly on the bottom of their enclosures waiting for fish to wander by. They are strictly carnivorous and should be offered a diet consisting of a variety of live fish. They require low pH in the 5.0 to 5.5 range to do well long-term in captivity. Many keepers use pH-lowering solutions available from a local tropical fish store. A keeper should also add plenty of live plants, branches, bark, and leaves to the water to more closely match the tannin-filled waters of their home.

Though drab in color, African Mud Turtles are hardy, omnivorous, and will readily breed in captivity. Photo by Russ Gurley.

African Mud Turtles (*Pelusios* species) are small (6" to 10") turtles that make hardy and alert captives. They are active baskers and will loudly plop into the water when a visitor approaches. They will quickly resurface to see if food is forthcoming. Food for African mud turtles includes a wide range of items, including commercial diets, insects, and fish. They will produce an obnoxious odor when disturbed, but captive-hatched specimens are less likely to exhibit this behavior.

Snake-necked Turtles (*Chelodina* species) are bizarre and delightful turtles that range in size from 8" to 24". They are found in Australia and Indonesia in nature.

Small Snake-necked turtles such as this Eastern Snake-necked Turtle, *Chelodina longicollis,* are somewhat delicate captives and will need close supervision. Photo by Russ Gurley.

Turtles

In proper captive conditions, young snake-necked turtles grow quickly and will need plenty of space. The small babies of most species are quite delicate and are definitely not for beginners unless the babies are well-started by a breeder. They need a thoughtful enclosure with warm, filtered water, plenty of live plants and decorations to feel secure, and most will only be interested in feeding on live blackworms, mosquito larvae, and small guppies. Juveniles, subadults, and adults will feed aggressively on mice, fish, and shrimp, and some species may be reluctant to eat commercial turtle food.

Pink-bellied Side-necked Turtles (*Emydura subglobosa*) are a beautiful, medium-sized (up to 10") species that has established well in captivity and captive-hatched babies are frequently available. The babies are no doubt some of the most beautiful baby turtles in the hobby and they thrive in a clean, warm environment. They feed eagerly on a variety of food including commercial turtle food and insects and they are especially fond of shrimp and krill.

Albino Pink-bellied Side-necks are some of the most beautiful turtles being produced in captivity. Courtesy of Paul vander Schouw. Photo by Russ Gurley.

Australia and Indonesia's **Pig-nosed Turtle** (*Carettochelys insculpta*) is a wonderful and mysterious freshwater turtle that is one of the most sought-after species in the hobby. They are herbivores, feeding on a variety of aquatic plants (*Valisneria* species being their favorite) in addition to romaine lettuce, kale, and other greens. They require large enclosures with plenty of clean, aerated water. Adult Pig-nosed Turtles will grow to 18" or more.

Young Pig-nosed Turtles thrive in enclosures that offer plenty of swimming space and warm, clean water. Photo by Russ Gurley.

Pig-nosed Turtles exhibit many features of their totally aquatic existence. Photo by Bill Love.

Giant Leaf Turtles (*Heosemys grandis*) are some of the hardiest and fastest-growing turtles being kept in captivity. They do, however, get larger than most keepers can accomodate. Photo by Russ Gurley.

The **Giant Leaf Turtle** (*Heosemys grandis*) is becoming more abundant in captivity as it is being successfully bred by several breeders who specialize in Asian species. The babies are hardy, tolerate a wide range of captive conditions, and eat aggressively on commercial turtle food, mice, earthworms, and salads composed of moist commercial turtle food and fruits and vegetables. They are alert and inquisitive and make wonderful pets. They do, however, grow quite large, with males reaching 16" to 18" and females 10" to 12".

Captive-hatched Chinese Thread Turtles, *Ocadia sinensis,* is are hardy captives. Photo by Russ Gurley.

Stripe-necked Turtles (*Ocadia sinensis*) are rare in nature. They were, however, established in captivity by several forward-thinking turtle breeders in the 1990s and have been bred in some numbers in the United States. The babies are a beautiful mossy green with rusty brown patches of color on their carapaces. They grow to 9" on a diet of aquatic plants and greens such as romaine lettuce, kale, carrot tops, other greens, and a low-fat/low-protein commercial turtle food.

Reeves Turtles (*Chinemys reevesi*) are small (8") turtles and are possibly one of the best pet turtles in the hobby. They are alert and inquisitive and will commonly become so tame that they will eat out of their keepers' fingers. They are tolerant of a wide range of captive conditions as long as they are kept in clean water

For a variety of reasons, Reeves Turtles are some of the best pet turtles in the hobby today. Photo by Russ Gurley.

Young, captive-hatched Reeves Turtles, *Chinemys reevesii*, will often "beg" for food when their keeper approaches. Photo by Russ Gurley.

with a secure basking spot and are offered a diet that consists of commercial turtle food, invertebrates, and small amounts of plant matter.

The **Spotted Turtle** (*Clemmys guttata*) is a beautiful black turtle with yellow spots. It is one of the most beautiful of North America's turtles. They

stay small (5" to 6") and will feed on a variety of food. They enjoy earthworms, redworms, crickets, strips of lean beef, commercial turtle food, etc. Spotted Turtles should be set up in a marshy, bog enclosure with a sand-peat substrate, large

Spotted Turtles thrive in captivity when given proper care. Photo by Russ Gurley.

flat water dish, and with plenty of live plants, cork bark, and leaves to provide some cover.

The **Wood Turtle** (*Actinemys insculpta*) is a handsome species that thrives in thoughtful captive enclosures. They have

An adult male Wood Turtle, *Actinemys insculpta*, searches its enclosure for an interesting meal. Photo by Russ Gurley.

proven to be
quite hardy and
prolific breeders
in captivity.
They grow to
11" and feed on
a wide variety
of food includ-
ing earthworms,
redworms,
crickets, strips
of lean beef,
and they will
enjoy an
occasional
(once a week)
large salad
consisting of

Young North American Wood Turtles thrive in captivity, becoming large, colorful adults. Photo by Russ Gurley.

a variety of chopped greens, vegetables, and fruit. Their enclosure should be similar to that of the Spotted Turtle, only a bit

Young box turtles such as this Eastern Box Turtle, *Terrapene carolina carolina*, are delicate, but will thrive in proper enclosures and with focused attention. Photo by Russ Gurley.

drier. We suggest a damp, forest environment with a damp sand-peat substrate, leaves, palm fronds, and bark and a large sloping paint tray or flat dish of clean water.

Box Turtles (*Terrapene* species) are found in a wide range of habitats. Most stay small, eat an omnivorous diet, and require a humid micro-habitat within their captive home. This is true of the desert species, plains species, and the humidity-loving forest species. They should be offered a humid shelter, especially as babies, in addition to a creative enclosure that features leaves, cork bark, and a variety of live plants.

Box Turtles will feed aggressively on a wide range of food including earthworms, crickets, pink mice, and most enjoy occasional treats of strawberries, cantaloupe, and

Captive-hatched box turtles are often quite tame and will take their favorite food items from a keeper's fingers. Photo by Russ Gurley.

other fruit. Their food items should be sprinkled with a vitamin and calcium mixture once a week (twice a week for young animals and egg-laying females).

Central and South American Wood Turtles (*Rhinoclemmys* species) require a damp substrate of peat moss and sand with the addition of lots of live plants, cork bark, and cypress mulch. They are omnivorous, feeding on animal (75%) and plant (25%) matter.

Central and South American Wood Turtles such as the Black Wood Turtle, *R. funerea*, (top) and the Ornate Wood Turtle, *R. p. manni*, (below) are rarely available as captive-hatched specimens. With some work and proper care, even the imported specimens do well in captivity. Photos by Russ Gurley.

They are especially fond of earthworms, crickets, commercial turtle foods, and banana, mango, and ripe cantaloupe.

The **Asian Box Turtles** (*Cuora* and *Cistoclemmys* species) are fascinating turtles that have a passionate and dedicated following in the turtle hobby. As many

Large outdoor enclosures make ideal homes for box turtles. Photo by Russ Gurley.

Cuora species such as this McCord's Box Turtle, *Cuora mccordi*, are often nervous captives and will spend a great deal of time under shelters or buried in the substrate. Photo by Russ Gurley.

of them are rare or extinct in their native China and Vietnam, they are receiving a great deal of attention from concerned turtle breeders. These are indeed some of the most threatened turtles on Earth. Captive-hatched babies are expensive, but have proven to be very hardy, reaching adulthood in as little as four years when

Modified stock tanks that offer clean water and multiple hiding spots are ideal homes for box turtles. Photo by Russ Gurley.

fed a healthy, balanced diet of invertebrates, commercial pelleted food, and some plant matter. Most species of Cuora will feed aggressively on earthworms, live fish, and small mice. The enclosure for most species should be a semi-aquatic habitat with clean, shallow water, a basking area, and a land section for exploring for food. Most Asian box turtles will thrive in large, semi-aquatic enclosures that offer cool, aerated water and plenty of hiding places. A basking spot in the 80° to 85° F range located at the entrance to one of their favorite hides is ideal.

SUGGESTED READING

Bartlett, R. D. and P. Bartlett. 1996. *Turtles and Tortoises: A Complete Pet Owner's Manual.* Barron's Educational Series, Inc. Hauppauge, N.Y.

de Vosjoli, P. 1992. *The General Care and Maintenance of Red-eared Sliders and Other Popular Freshwater Turtles.* Advanced Vivarium Systems, California, USA.

de Vosjoli, P. and R. Klingenberg. 1996. *The Box Turtle Manual.* Advanced Vivarium Systems, California, USA.

Ernst, C. H. and R. W. Barbour. 1989. *Turtles of the World.* Smithsonian Institution Press.

Ernst, C. H., J. Lovich, and R. W. Barbour. 1994. *Turtles of the United States and Canada.* Smithsonian Institution Press.

Ferri, V. 2002. *Turtles & Tortoises.* Firefly Books, Buffalo, New York. 255 pp.

Grenard, S. 1994. *Medical Herpetology.* NG Publishing Reptile & Amphibian Magazine Pottsville, PA.

Gurley, R. 2003. *Keeping and Breeding Freshwater Turtles.* LIVING ART publishing, Ada, OK.

Gurley, R. 2004. *Baby Turtles.* LIVING ART publishing. Ada, OK.

Highfield, A. 1996. *Practical Encyclopedia of Keeping and Breeding Tortoises and Freshwater Tortoises.* Carapace Press. England.

Iverson, J. B. 1992. *A Revised Checklist with Distribution Maps of the Turtles of the World.* Iverson Publishing, Richmond, IN.

Pritchard, P. C. H. 1979. *Encyclopedia of Turtles.* T.F.H. Publications, Inc. New Jersey, 895 p.

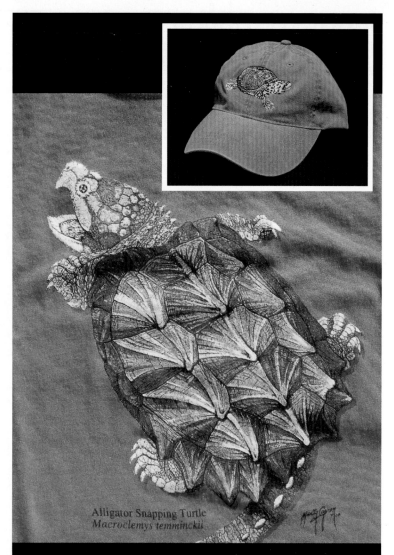

Alligator Snapping Turtle
Macroclemys temminckii